THE LEEDS, CASTL
PONTEFRACT JUN
RAILWAY

THE LEDSTON BRANCH

Ron Rockett

Published by Martin Bairstow, 53 Kirklees Drive, Farsley, Leeds
Printed by The Amadeus Press, Cleckheaton, West Yorkshire

Origins

The branch line between Castleford and Garforth was conceived as the Leeds Castleford & Pontefract Junction Railway and was intended to exploit the area's coal reserves. It had no pretensions to main-line status – its business was coal, which it carried in great quantities as long as it was there to be moved. When at last the fortunes of the coal industry waned, the railway faded away with it, but for most of its existence, the branch was busy and even managed to support a meagre passenger service for some seventy years. The story of the LCPJR is typical of dozens of backwaters of Britain's once extensive railway system.

The very northern edge of the Yorkshire coalfield lies just to the north of the river Aire between Castleford and Leeds. Coal was being won on the Lowther Estate at Swillington before 1700 and the industry gradually expanded during the first half of the 18th century. A steam pumping engine was in use locally and by 1764 a wagon-way was known to be in place down to the river. At Allerton Bywater the 'modern' colliery was opened in 1875, but shallow seams had been worked on the site for the previous hundred years, again with wagon-way links to the Aire. In these early years waterways were the only reliable means of moving coal in bulk, but they had their limitations.

The first major railway in the area, promoted at a meeting in March 1829, was an attempt by merchants in Leeds and businessmen in Hull to capitalise on the new form of transport. Thus the Leeds & Selby Railway opened in December 1834 and was welcomed in the Garforth area not least by Oliver Gascoign, an influential local landowner who was elected to the board. To the south, the York & North Midland Railway was promoted by one George Hudson to link his home city of York with Normanton, where there was to be a junction with a line coming up from London via the Midlands. The Y&NMR, passing through Castleford, opened in July 1840. The L&S was absorbed by the Y&NM which became a constituent of the North Eastern Railway on its formation in 1854, by which time railways were well-established as the form of transport powering the Industrial Revolution.

The area between these two railways comprised a rich coalfield which was entirely reliant on water transport; the Aire and Calder Navigation was a progressive company with its continual enlargement of locks, and innovations such as compartment boats and steam tugs, but it still suffered from the draw-backs inherent in its kind – it was slow and could not easily serve locations away from valley bottoms. If the Kippax-Ledston area was to keep up with progress elsewhere, then a railway was required.

Seen from the end of Ledston Station platform, 37249 draws a train of well filled hoppers out of Allerton Bywater Colliery in October 1983. This was one of the last old style trains before the "merry go rounds" took over. Note the excellent condition of the "main line" heading north to St Aidans.

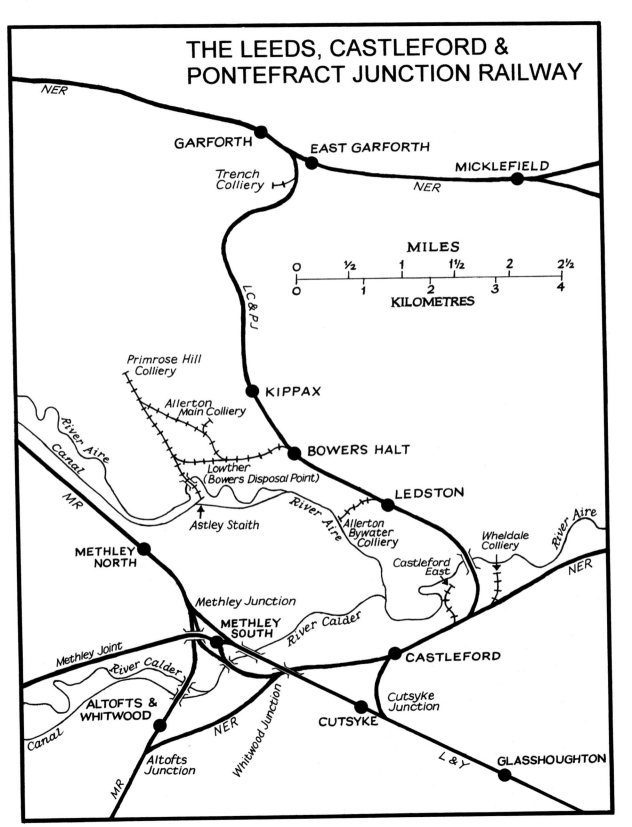

THE LEEDS, CASTLEFORD & PONTEFRACT JUNCTION RAILWAY

A group of local landowners, coal owners and businessmen therefore engaged John Fraser and Walter Bentley to survey a route for an independent railway between Garforth and Castleford with a continuation to the L&YR at Cutsyke thus giving access via that railway to Goole. The plans were submitted to Parliament in November 1872. Objections came from the NER on the grounds that the proposed route was in the middle of their territory and thus if anyone should build a railway, it was themselves. The obvious counter to this argument was that they had had ample opportunity for twenty years.

A more understandable objection was raised by the A&C Navigation, which stood to lose a lot of business, but canal companies had for fifty years not been able to deny accusations of lack of speed and flexibility. It was also not in the Waterway's favour that coal on a journey to London, for example, was transhipped up to eleven times as against four times by rail, excessive handling resulting in a significant reduction in quality. Finally the A&C's argument was not helped by the revelation that one of its directors, Sir Charles Lowther, had himself invested £4,000 in the proposed railway.

Royal Assent was given to the LCPJR Bill on 21 July 1873 and construction was able to proceed. The Company was authorised to raise £120,000 in shares and £40,000 in loans. Only 25% of the shares had been taken up when the NER turned from objector to saviour when it offered to subscribe the remaining capital in exchange for three seats on the Board, with a view to eventually acquiring the LCPJR entirely. As a result, certain amendments were made to the route, especially at the southern end where the line would now run into the NER station at Castleford instead of on a separate route alongside.

Construction began in April 1875, contractors Benton and Woodiwiss being experienced railway builders whose work included sections of the far more difficult Settle & Carlisle Line. No problems were encountered and the NER took over powers of construction on 13 July 1876, with the buildings and signalling completed to the then standard designs of that company. It is not known whether the LCPJR directors originally envisaged a passenger service – probably not, since potential traffic locally was minimal. However, once the NER became involved it made sense to inaugurate a service from their Leeds station to the towns of Castleford and Pontefract. A couple of basic stations on the branch catered for whatever local patronage was forthcoming, and at each a small goods shed was also provided.

Coal trains began working over the branch from 8 April 1878 followed by passenger services on 12 August, terminating at Castleford but extended to Pontefract Baghill from 1 April 1880.

The Railway was built to carry coal. It was fed by the internal colliery lines. 0 - 6 - 0ST "Astley" at Fleakingley Beck on the Allerton Main system in Summer 1969.
(Stuart Carmichael)

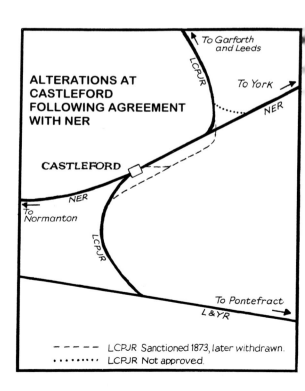

ALTERATIONS AT CASTLEFORD FOLLOWING AGREEMENT WITH NER

To Garforth and Leeds

To York

NER

CASTLEFORD

NER

To Normanton

LCPJR

LCPJR

To Pontefract

L&YR

– – – – LCPJR Sanctioned 1873, later withdrawn.

·········· LCPJR Not approved.

The Route Described

Castleford East Junction, looking towards York, about 1963. Taken from Old Station Signal Box.

The Ledston branch is the single track heading towards Wheldale Colliery in the distance. Sunk in 1869/70 this pit had access from both the main line and the branch, but in January 1965 Wheldale Box was closed and the main line connection removed. The colliery survived until 1987.

The two large chimneys to the right belong to the Healdfield and Redhill brickworks.

Castleford 'East branch' curves off to the extreme left, formerly serving several industrial premises, the last of which abandoned rail in the early 1970s (Hickson & Welch chemical manufacturers). East branch had no direct access and could be reached only via a headshunt off the Ledston line. !474

Inner Junction signal box once stood where the Ledston branch turned away northwards (see map). It was shown on 1908 O.S. maps but had disappeared by the 1933 edition.

Easily the most impressive structure on the branch is the bridge over the River Aire. With a central span of approx. 200ft and ten spans each side of 30ft, the total length is around 800ft with clearance of 31ft above normal river level. It was built to take double track though the second track was never laid and for many years now has carried a water main instead.

This is not the bridge as originally planned; it was intended at first to provide a brick structure 23ft high, with a 80ft arch and two of 40ft. The reason for the change is not known, but the unstable marshy ground was probably the deciding factor.

The gradient profile shows 1 in 144 approaching the bridge from the north, though with colliery subsidence rife in the area, these are theoretical figures and more often than not bear little relation to reality. With the track eventually being in very poor condition there was a general speed restriction of 10mph – not always adhered to, though it seems no derailments occurred.

The branch was split into four sections for operational purposes, but after the closure of Kippax signal box this became three: Garforth to Bowers, Bowers to Ledston, and Ledston to Castleford Old Sta. Nowhere could two passenger trains pass each other but apart from when the line was used for diversions, the sparse service didn't require it. Goods trains could be shunted out of the way at Ledston and Bowers when necessary.

Ledston

Ledston station was near the colliery village of Allerton Bywater and on the NER architect's drawings it seems the original intention was to name it as such. However, the line opened at a time when the NER was trying to eliminate confusion caused by duplicated names and as it already had an

37083 framed between the girders of the Aire Bridge on 19 January 1984.

Having negotiated the central span, 37249 still has to cross the outer section of the bridge, which carries the line clear of the flood plain. This is the daily working of coal from Allerton Bywater on 11 October 1983.

In August 1985, a class 56 treads warily over the river with coal from St Aidans opencast site. The official gradient profile seems to have been overtaken by subsidence.

Another class 56 approaching the bridge with loaded wagons from Allerton Bywater in January 1990.

Ledston signal box was resited on the platform in 1910. This made it easier to have it manned by a porter - signalman though, from staff vacancy lists, this appears not to have happened until about 1930. The box closed in January 1988.

Ledston Station, after closure to regular passenger service, still intact and in use.
(Peter Cookson)

Ledston Station, looking towards Castleford in May 1957
(P B Booth/ N E Stead collection)

The only form of station lighting ever known at Ledston and Kippax, was a North Eastern pattern oil lantern.

Allerton on its system, and maybe in deference to the owners of the Hall, it was decided to name the new station 'Ledstone' – after the small village a mile away. From 2 July 1915 this was modified to Ledston.

The short single platform was more than adequate for the train service provided – typically a G5 0-4-4T and four coaches. The staff, some of whom lived in the railway houses to the right, had plenty of time to tend the gardens.

In 1911, from a population of 2500, 15208 tickets were issued. Apart from coal, the main products handled were ashes/cinders of which 27377 tons were forwarded that year.

The goods shed closed on 30 September, 1963 – it can be seen in the background of both photographs – and in 2003 is the only building still in existence.

The station buildings at both Kippax and Ledston were to a single-platform no-frills design produced by the NER's own architects, variations appearing throughout the north east at the time. Built of local red brick, two wings end-on to the platform were joined by another section incorporating a verandah with glazed roof. Even in such a modest building it was still felt necessary to incorporate three separate waiting rooms. The southern wing also accommodated the booking office with a distinctive

Ledston was still largely intact in April 1979.

(Alan Young)

Just before demolition in 1992.

By 1997, the one remaining building was the small goods shed. Last used for its original purpose in September 1963, it continues to serve a builders merchant.

bay window containing a desk used by the Stationmaster who thus had a good view of his domain.

Before the first War, signalling alterations resulted in the replacement of the original signalboxes by a platform-mounted wooden design built onto the south wing and covering the bay window. Otherwise there were no other alterations before closure.

Other buildings were typically North Eastern, from the weighbridge and tiny goods shed to the row of terraced houses for railway staff.

Bowers Halt was a late addition to the passenger facilities on the Ledston branch. Opened on 15 December 1934 it was a minimal wooden structure accommodating only a couple of coaches and was presumably intended to cater for the new housing being built nearby. The signal box is, unusually for the NER, all-wood and the track diverging from the 'main line' served various pits including Allerton main. 'Halt' was dropped from the station name from 3rd May 1937.

Kippax

The railway, climbing towards Garforth, followed a shallow valley with Kippax village occupying higher ground to the northeast, some ³/₄ mile away – in fact the station was nearer to Great Preston. Both villages were largely of 19th century colliery housing, though Kippax's origins go much further back, with its Saxon church and the remains of a castle.

Whereas only two postcard views of Castleford station seem to have survived, Kippax is better documented. The style of nameboard was replaced from 1901 by a chocolate and white enamel variety. An early type of NER signal with the lamp half way down the post can be seen on the right, and behind it the signalbox in its original position.

The station buildings at Ledston and Kippax were identical but in addition Kippax boasted a water tank, and the goods shed and loading dock were at the opposite end of the platform. At both stations a distinctive bay window graced the southernmost gable ends.

In common with nearly all stations in the 19th century, Kippax had its own stationmaster. In 1881 it was a John Henry Whitelock and between 1893 and 1901 William Robinson Tebb.

In 1911, from a surrounding population of 5500, 44421 tickets were issued. The main commodity handled by the goods yards was sand and gravel (956 tons) which came from a small quarry served by a single siding a few hundred yards to the north of the station.

Bowers Halt, photographed in May 1957 from the angle between the main line from Garforth (left) and the branch to Allerton Main collieries (right). The water column was the only such facilty on the line.

(P B Booth/ N E Stead collection)

Inside Ledston signal box.
(John Holroyd)

Architects drawings, side and rear, for the identical goods sheds at Kippax and Ledston.

Rail level

End elevations of the station buildings which appear on the next page.

Kippax Station in the 1950s, closed to regular passenger traffic, but otherwise fully operational. The large water tower had no crane for locomotives. What was its purpose? *(Peter Cookson)*

An earlier view when the signal box was still in operation. Signals 13 and 10 gave a choice of route, by the main line or goods loop, respectively. *(Martin Bairstow collection)*

Kippax station, identical to Ledston, before the signal box was placed on the platform in 1910.

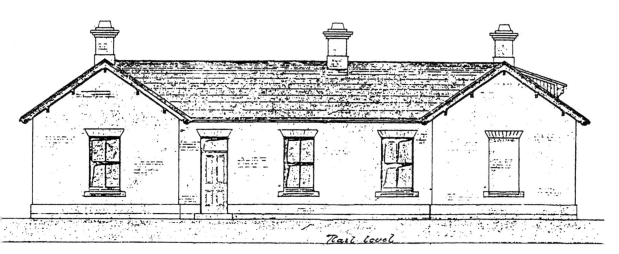

The original drawings are headed "Kippax and Allerton Bywater Stations" but the latter name is altered manually to read "Ledston".

About 1950, a Q6 0 - 8 - 0 shunts the breakdown crane at Ledston during renewal of the road bridge from which the photograph was taken.

(J Bouldon)

The area between the Aire Bridge and Ledston Station was susceptible to flooding but rarely was the damage as bad as this. In January 1982, heavy rain was followed by severe frost. A quick thaw then led to this washout behind the NCB workshops.

Guaranteed excursions, where the organisers bore the risk, were a significant source of traffic. The class 40 Diesel should be adequate power for this working mens club excursion, climbing from Kippax towards Garforth, about 1962. *(M Baldwin)*

With its sanders going, "Jubilee" class No 45589 "Gwalior" struggles in atrocious weather on the up grade between Bowers and Kippax, about 1963.
(M Baldwin)

Trench Pit, near Garforth was served by a siding from Inner Junction signal box. It closed in 1930.

"Deltic" No D9010, as yet un-named, coming off the branch at Garforth on 7 April 1963 with the diverted 10.10 am from Kings Cross to Leeds. Signalman Bob Barton has collected the single line tablet.
(J M Rayner)

All sign of the branch has gone as a class 158 passes the same spot on 12 February 2000 with a westbound "Trans Pennine Express".

Garforth in NER days. Today the goods facilities have gone but the passenger station retains much the same appearance. The pre 1928 East Junction signal box is just visible.

"Jubilee" class 4 - 6 - 0 No 45593 "Kolhapur" in the outskirts of Garforth with a special on 22 April 1967. The train was chartered by the Middleton Railway Trust from Leeds to Derby Works via Castleford and Doncaster.

(G W Morrison)

A K3 2 - 6 -0 waiting to depart Kippax with an excursion for Bridlington in July 1959.

(Peter Sunderland)

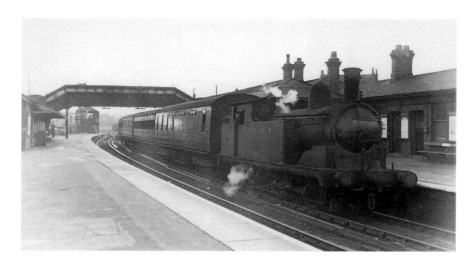

Sporting its new BR number but with LNER still on the side tanks, G5 0-4-4 T No 67301 is ready to leave Castleford for Leeds via Garforth about 1948.

The same K3 hauled excursion calls at Ledston. It will run round at Castleford, then continue chimney first to Bridlington.

(Peter Sunderland)

A returning excursion, between Bowers and Kippax, double headed by LNER class B1 No 61086 and LMS "Jubilee" class No 45581 "Bihar & Orissa"

(M Baldwin)

Passing Allerton Bywater on 26 April 1958 with an Ian Allan excursion, class A1 "Pacific" No 60157 "Great Eastern".

(Peter Sunderland)

Bringing up the rear of the Ian Allan Special is an ex "Devon Belle" Pullman Observation Car.

(Peter Sunderland)

Passing Garforth signal box with the Newcastle to Red Bank empty newspaper vans on 8 June 1960. "Black Five" No 45233 pilots No 45156 "Ayrshire Yeomanry". The Castleford line branches to the right, initially as double track. *(Peter Cookson)*

Fairburn 2 - 6 -4T No 42073 has the 2.30 pm from Pontefract Baghill to Leeds Central at Castleford on 3 April 1961. This train has used the short section of LC&PJ line from Cutsyke Junction. It will proceed to Leeds via the Methley Joint. *(David Holmes)*

Long after closure of the Ledston branch, Castleford Station remains in business, albeit unstaffed. 141119, since withdrawn, is on a stopping service to Sheffield in August 1991. The West Yorkshire PTE wants to see a ticket office reintroduced at Castleford.

(Martin Bairstow)

Garforth has fared better with the main building, seen here from the outside, still in use. The half hourly stopping service is complemented by an hourly semi fast giving six departures per hour.

(Martin Bairstow)

The PTE once spoke of wanting a station at South Garforth, to be reached by a short stretch of rebuilt Ledston branch. That aspiration seems to have been satisfied by East Garforth, opened on the main line in 1987. 158901 calls with a York to Manchester Victoria service on 14 August 1991.

(Martin Bairstow)

Goods Traffic

Apart from the pick-up goods, freight traffic was almost exclusively coal either for export or for home markets, and was taken off the branch in both directions. At first the NER worked it all, but from 1 June 1899 that bound for Goole via Knottingley began to be worked throughout by the L&Y. Previously the NER hauled it as far as Pontefract Monkhill.

Similarly, the NER worked southbound coal to Normanton using its own locomotives based at the MR shed there, but by the 1950s, probably as a result of the transfer of Normanton to the N.E. Region, LMS locos were frequently used throughout.

The North Eastern Railway and its successors were not the only companies to operate railways in the area. The several collieries connected to the branch had their own railway systems, some with extensive (and intensive) operations. As well as feeding coal onto the Ledston branch, they moved a substantial portion of output to staiths on the Aire and Calder Navigation, and spoil away to the tips. They had their own locomotives and drivers and a large fleet of wagons for both main-line and internal use.

Tramways are known to have existed in the 1770s, from local coal pits to the River Aire. Astley, owned by the Lowthers but worked by Fenton & Smith was making use of one; the same partnership leased Allerton Bywater workings and by 1775 operated a tramway there. These would have been horse-worked but steam locos must have been used at some collieries before the arrival of the Ledston branch – T&RW Bower's Allerton Main Collieries purchased No. 136, a Hudswell-Clarke 0-4-0ST in 1873.

A coal train emerging from the loop at Allerton Main Box, Bowers Halt on the left.
None of the signal boxes on the branch could actually pass two trains, an indication that most freight movements were to, from or between intermediate points on the line. Through freight trains would have required dedicated paths with an assurance that they were not going to meet traffic coming the other way. If two trains did approach one of the signal boxes from opposite directions, a perfectly legal movement, then one of them would have to be shunted off the main line as there was nowhere else to go. The intermediate boxes were block posts but not passing loops.

Heavy power waiting to take the Ledston branch. 9F 2 - 10 - 0 Nos 92173 and 92085 wait the right away from Castleford Station with oil tanks for Hunslet East via Garforth in May 1967.

WD 2 - 8- 0 No 90427 makes a noisy exit from Bowers Row sidings, about 1960. Because of the gradient, trains were often divided to get away from the sidings, then re-formed at Bowers Halt. *(M Baldwin)*

The morning pick up goods at Kippax behind Q6 0 - 6 - 0 No 63417 on 1 September 1964.

(David Holmes)

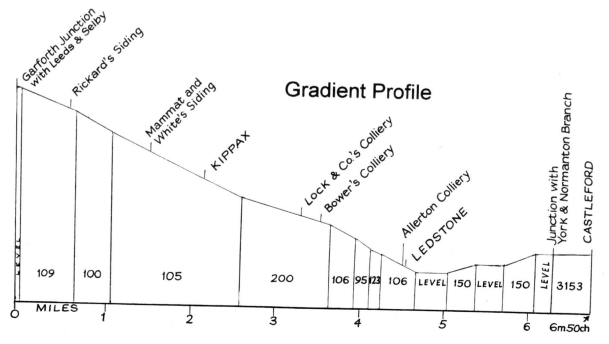

Gradient Profile

The daily grind - heavy coal trains on steep gradients were the order of the day for almost a century. Already more than 50 years old, work stained Q6 0 - 8 - 0 No 63424 clambers at walking pace towards Garforth about 1960.

(M Baldwin)

A Normanton based WD 2 - 8 - 0 passing Ledston with coal heading for the marshalling yards at Normanton.

(M Baldwin)

Another Normanton engine, ex LMS 4F 0 - 6 - 0 No 44336 on a similar working with what appears to be a heavier load, a stern test for the smaller loco.

(M Baldwin)

Signalling

Single line security was achieved by staff and ticket, from opening of the line until 1 December 1898, when electric staffs were introduced. The sections were:

- Garforth Inner Junction to Kippax
- Kippax to Allerton Main
- Allerton Main to Ledston
- Ledston to Castleford Inner Junction

The electric staffs were replaced by Tyers No 6 tablets in 1923.

It was common practice for a single track branch to leave the main line by a conventional double track junction, then reduce to single line at an Inner Junction box, perhaps mile to the branch. This arrangement was labour intensive and tended to be superseded in the 20th century.

When Castleford Inner Junction signal box was destroyed by fire in the 1920s, the LNER decided not to rebuild it, but to incorporate its working into that of Old Stationbox. This involved the introduction of a system then new to British railways. The section between Inner Junction and Ledston had been worked under the electric tablet regulations. In principle, it would have been possible to dispense with Inner Junction signal box and still retain token working but this would have required subsidiary instruments at the junction with the single line. Delays to traffic would have resulted from operation by loco crews. Traffic requirements were such that token working between Old Station and Ledston would not have been feasible.

The system thus adopted in 1926 was an intermittent track circuit which proved cheaper to instal and maintain as well as more efficient in operation than the alternatives. It also demonstrated its suitability for the safe operation of bi-directional or reversible working on other lines.

The three sets of connections at Inner Junction were beyond the limit of mechanical operation. So they were equipped with low-voltage high-speed battery motors, the time required for the complete

The down fixed distant at Allerton Main in 1969. After the passenger closure, the distant signals on the branch were no longer "pulled off". *(John Holroyd)*

movement being 3^1/$_2$ to 5 seconds.

At Garforth, the West, East and Inner Junction boxes were all replaced on 22 April 1928 by one 60

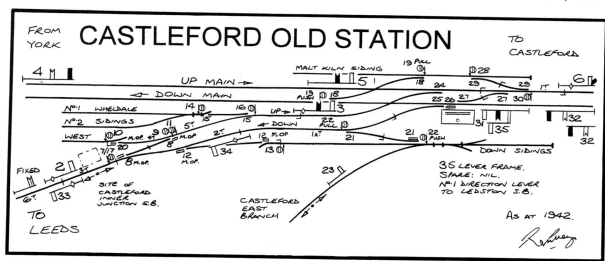

FROM YORK
CASTLEFORD OLD STATION
TO CASTLEFORD

As at 1942.

lever box which worked the former Inner Junction by a motor operated point. The tablet section became Garforth to Kippax, Garforth to Allerton Main after kippax box closed on 16 April 1939. This latter move scarcely affected line capacity as Kippax could never pass two trains anyway. Garforth signal box remained in use until November 1984 when the Leeds power box area was extended.

Allerton Main box was dispensed with in August 1970, after the line had closed as a through route.

The truncated branch then functioned under "one engine in steam" regulations beyond Ledston, where the signal box remained open until 19 January 1988.

Old Station box, Castleford closed on 19 August 1973, after which the junction for Ledston was controlled from Castleford Station box. This in turn closed in 1997, when the Castleford area went under the control of a new box at Castleford Gates. But, by that time the Ledston branch was already out of use.

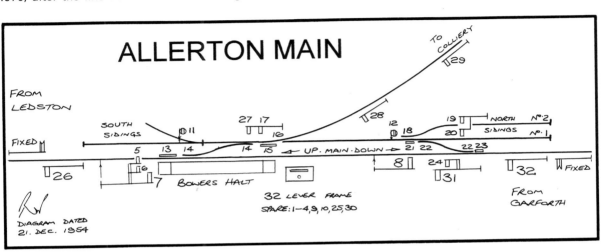

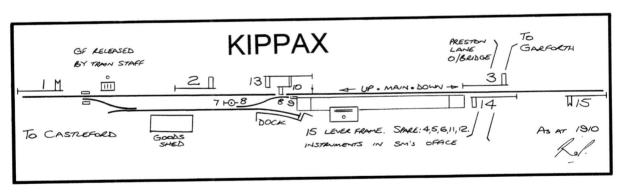

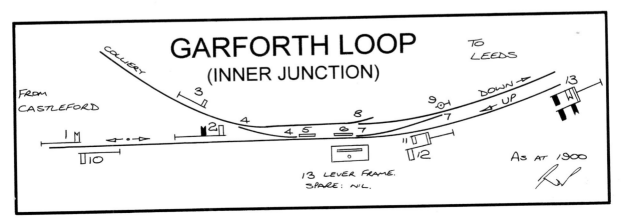

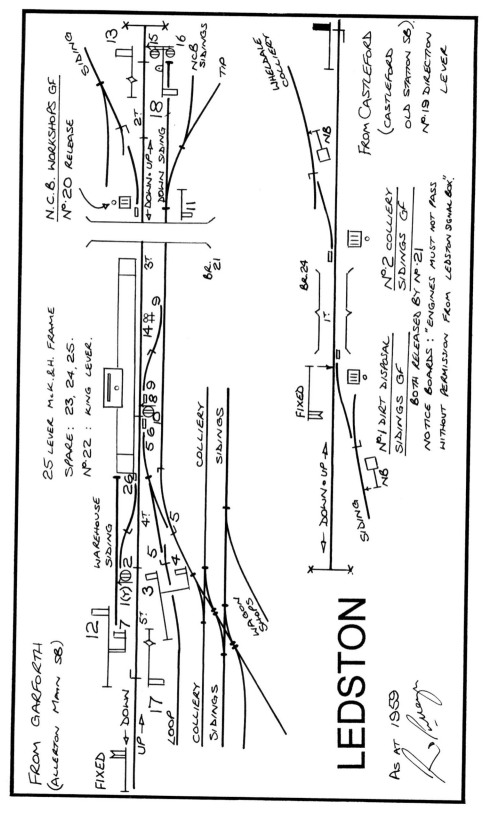

LEDSTON

As at 1959

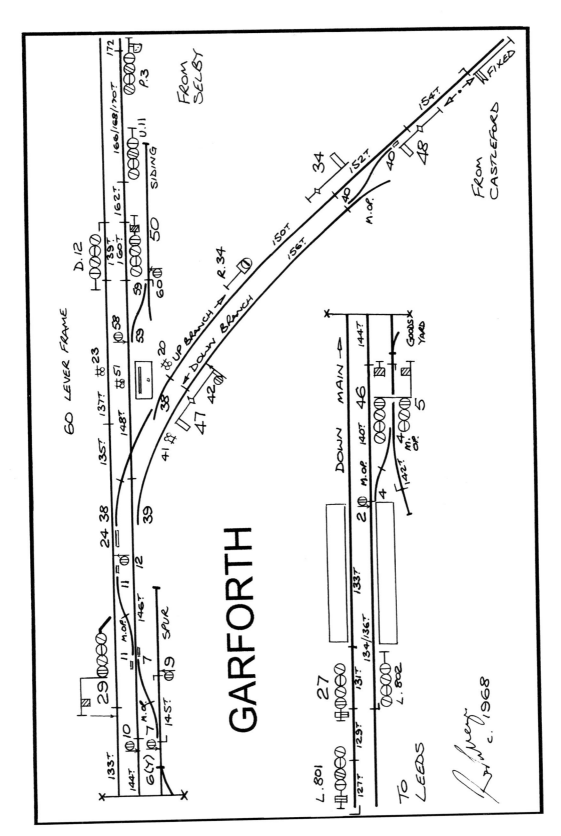

GARFORTH

60 LEVER FRAME

D.12

FROM SELBY

FROM CASTLEFORD

DOWN MAIN

GOODS YARD

TO LEEDS

c. 1968

Allerton Bywater Colliery

The fleet of Airedale Collieries wagons appears to have been specially marshalled for this photograph taken from the spoil tips, looking south in the 1920s.

The 'modern' colliery was sunk in 1875 on a site which had been worked for more than a century. Owners were the Silkstone and Haigh Moor Coal Co. who enlarged the mine in 1910 and then in February 1921 merged with several other local collieries to form Airedale Collieries Ltd. As the pit grew, so did its railway system, spread out alongside the Ledston branch with a line to the staiths at right-angles. It produced gas, steam, industrial and household grades of good-quality coal, and after modernisation in 1978 its output for a workforce of some 1240 men was in the region of 880,000 tons annually. Eventually as markets shrank, its only outlet of any importance was to power stations, though its coal had to be blended with poorer-quality product from other mines before it could be used.

The colliery eventually closed in March 1992 by which time it was one of the last deep mines in Yorkshire.

Though the establishment of the national railway network – and the opening of the LCPJR in particular – enabled local collieries to expand, much coal still used the Aire & Calder Navigation, especially to reach Goole and Hull for export. The A & CN, under its engineer W.H. Bartholomew pioneered steam tugs and compartment boats (known as Tom Puddings) from the 1860s and continued to compete effectively in the transport of coal. Internal railways connected the colliery to its staiths where there were various ways of unloading wagons. At Allerton this involved end-tipping though others used rotary tipplers or hopper wagons with bottom doors.

To avoid undue breakage, manouverable chutes poured the coal into waiting barges.

Advantage was taken of the branch's capacity for double track to lay a line to sidings serving wagon storage and stockyards, used by both colliery and railway company but owned by the latter and controlled from Ledston signal box.

The site of the colliery was somewhat restricted and eventually ran out of space for spoil tipping by the late 1970s. It was decided to use the marshy land alongside the river downstream for this purpose and the track to the stockyards threw off a long siding used solely by colliery trains, eventually extending almost two miles as the spoil was spread out. En route it passed under the B.R. line beneath the Aire Bridge. Here a short-lived connection was put in, allowing spoil trains access to Allerton tips via the B.R. bridge.

The spoil run was quite steeply graded beyond the Aire Bridge and a novel form of banking developed – presumably without official blessing. A descending train of empties would wait in the passing loop; as a loaded train passed, the loco off the empties would leave its wagons and chase after the ascending train to give it a push – without stopping – before returning to its empties. This apparently was a local Allerton agreement – Wheldale men had to struggle up unaided!

These wagons, known as dirt cans or Jubilee wagons, were primitive but sturdy side-tipplers of 10-ton capacity used to carry spoil to the tips. They received rough treatment in appalling conditions on trackwork that was rough even by colliery standards. Casualties were simply heaved off the track or lay where they fell until rescue could be attempted, and towards the end, it often wasn't. Some ended their days at the bottom of slurry lagoons.

In the early 1980s when the branch was lightly used, it was decided to allow spoil trains from Wheldale Colliery access to Allerton's tips, using NCB locos and drivers 'passed' for B.R. running. This brought the very rare sight of 'dirt cans' in use on B.R. metals, and continued almost until Wheldale's closure in 1987.

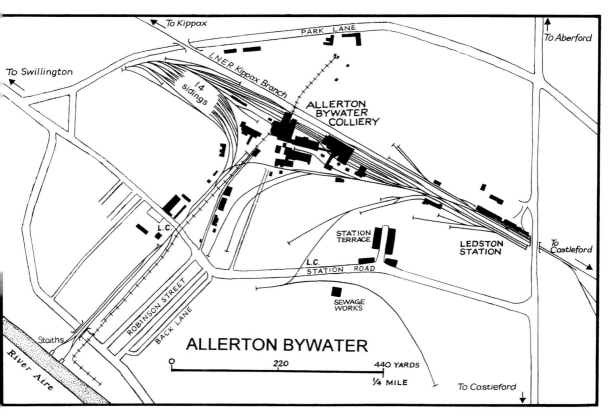

No 10, a brand new 0 - 6 -0 Diesel from Hudswell Clarke, alongside Ledston Station in July 1959.

(Peter Sunderland)

Track work at Allerton Bywater in 1969, guaranteed to derail just about anything.
(John Holroyd)

0 - 4 - 0 Diesel No 45 rusting away at Allerton Bywater in June 1983. *(A J Booth)*

An Airedale Collieries publicity photograph shows the Allerton Staiths with a "train" of loaded "Tom Puddings" poised alongside. Just visible is a horse drawing a narrow gauge tub, possibly removing spoil.

The staiths becoming derelict in April 1972.

ACKNOWLEDGEMENTS

The daily life of the Ledston Branch was recorded by only a few photographers so I am in debt to those who have made their efforts available, and to those who have shared their memories of the line, particularly Martin and John Baldwin and Jack Collins. Those who have encouraged and bullied me into print include Peter Cookson, Tony Ross and John Teasdale.

Much help has been afforded by the Industrial Railway Society and the North Eastern Railway Association, both of which can be contacted for information on their respective subjects.

Richard Pulleyn drew the signal diagrams and Alan Young lettered the maps. Uncredited photographs are my own or from my collection.

Ron Rockett
Castleford
October 2003

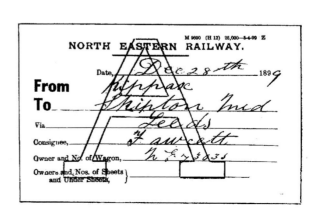

Hunslet "Vanguard" diesels Nos 45 and 47 passing the NCB Central Workshops with loaded spoil wagons.

No 47 leaves the head of its own train......

.... And provides banking assistance to an uphill train under the Aire Bridge.

An NCB diesel crossing the Aire Bridge with Wheldale spoil empties on 11 October 1983.

The extent of the tips can be seen in the background.

NCB "dirt cans" used the BR line until the closure of Wheldale Colliery in 1987.

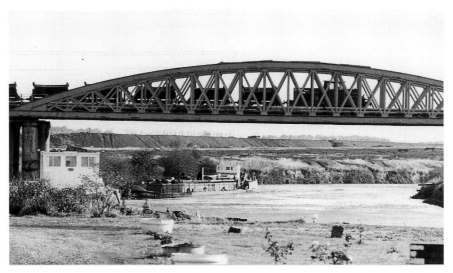

Allerton Main Collieries

The new (1957) loco shed at Primrose Hill Colliery on 6 October 1968. 0 - 6 - 0ST No S116, on the left, shows signs of accident damage to the bunker. Just visible, behind "Jubilee", is "Primrose Hill No 2" which now hauls passenger trains on the Embsay & Bolton Abbey Railway.

(Martin Bairstow collection)

The most extensive colliery railway system was that owned by T&RW Bower, known as Allerton Main Collieries, which gave its name to the signal box controlling the NER access to their sidings just to the south of Kippax. In an area where coal had been won for centuries, by 1831 a tramway was operating from pits at Swillington and Little Preston to Astley Staiths on the River Aire.

Lowther pit was sunk by Bowers in the 1870s and a railway built from the Ledston branch to connect with it, and extended to the Old Engine Pit, but the latter seems to have soon become worked out. A branch turned off northwards to serve Victoria Colliery then onwards to join the 1831 tramway from Astley Staith to Fleakingley Beck which was then upgraded to a conventional railway. Primrose Hill Colliery opened in 1893 served by a new direct line from Victoria, and ten years later Fleakingley Beck shaft was modernised and its coal went down to Victoria by rope-worked narrow-gauge tramway. The washery for all three collieries was at Victoria.

Colliery names can be a little confusing – often a colliery had two or three shafts or pits, each with a different name and usually an unofficial name as well. Thus Victoria Colliery had two shafts – Victoria (also known as Johnny Pit) and Albert (known as Star Pit). Along with Fleakingley Beck and Primrose Hill, the whole operation was known as Allerton Main Collieries. As an added complication Victoria was commonly known as Allerton Main! T&RW Bower became a subsidiary of Pease & Co in 1919 and then (along with Allerton Bywater, Fryston and Wheldale) as Airedale Collieries from 1940 to Nationalisation in 1947.

Lowther Colliery closed June 1948 but the extensive sidings were retained as exchange sidings between B.R. and the N.C.B. By 1949 Primrose Hill

had been modernised and this enabled Fleakingley Beck to be closed. As a result from 1015 men producing 6 to 7000 tons of coal per week, 886 men were getting 12000 tons.

Further improvements saw a new washer (or "Coal Preparation Plant") installed at Primrose Hill and the ancient contraption at Victoria dismantled. The loco shed for the system was also replaced by a new one at Primrose Hill when Victoria pit finally closed in 1957.

Thus by 1960 only Primrose Hill remained, but with considerable railway activity. Spoil from the pit was being dumped from various short-lived sidings off the Astley Staiths line; the staiths were kept busy loading Tom Puddings and barges; and coal destined for rail delivery was worked down to the exchange sidings at Bowers. Here there were three roads for outgoing coal – one each for Leeds, Normanton and Gascoign Wood. Somewhat strangely, coal also came into Primrose Hill for washing from other collieries, notably Prince of Wales at Pontefract and Allerton Bywater, at the rate of a train a day.

Primrose Hill closed on November 13th 1969 but the washery continued until 25th March 1971 when all rail operations ceased.

However, this was not the end of the story – opencast mining had begun in the area in 1958 and the southern half of the old Lowther sidings were designated to handle this production. They were operated by Wm. Pepper & Co., later by Hargreaves. Opencasting increased until virtually the whole area became part of the giant St. Aidans mine which continued to send coal out to power stations from Bowers Disposal Point, as the terminal became known. This ended suddenly when the mine accidentally flooded in February 1987.

Coal from other collieries was brought into Primrose Hill for washing, either because their own facilities were out of action or were unable to keep up with the volume of production. By February 1970, washing was the only commercial activity remaining at Primrose Hill.

(John Holroyd)

S134 approaches Astley Staiths over the "Iron Bridge" of 1831, which originally carried a colliery tramroad. Unless the second wagon is a purchase from BR, it has been borrowed to work on the internal system.

(C Shepherd)

Hunslet 0 - 6 - 0ST "Jubilee" crossing the road near Astley with a train of empties returning from the spoil tip to Primrose Hill Colliery during Summer 1969. *(Stuart Carmichael)*

One of the Hunslet 0 - 6 - 0 saddle tanks working Astley Staiths.

(M Baldwin)

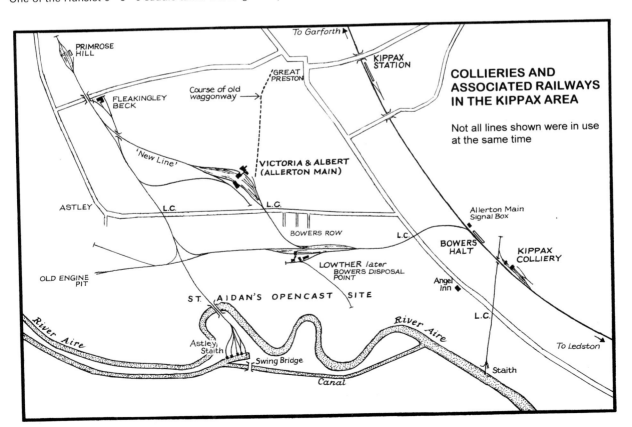

To Garforth

PRIMROSE HILL

KIPPAX STATION

'GREAT PRESTON'

FLEAKINGLEY BECK

Course of old waggonway

COLLIERIES AND ASSOCIATED RAILWAYS IN THE KIPPAX AREA

Not all lines shown were in use at the same time

'New Line'

VICTORIA & ALBERT (ALLERTON MAIN)

ASTLEY   L.C.   L.C.

Allerton Main Signal Box

BOWERS ROW   L.C.

OLD ENGINE PIT

BOWERS HALT

KIPPAX COLLIERY

LOWTHER *later* BOWERS DISPOSAL POINT

Angel Inn

ST. AIDAN'S OPENCAST SITE

L.C.

River Aire

River Aire

To Ledston

Astley Staith

Swing Bridge

Canal

Staith

Hunslet 0 - 6 - 0ST "Jubilee" shunts loaded coal wagons at Primrose Hill Colliery on 16 March 1968. Sister engine No S134 stands with empties.

(C Shepherd)

St Aidans opencast site on 4 September 1986. Bowers is in the distance, behind the crane.

Workshops

After Nationalisation in 1947, the new No. 8 Area (Castleford) of the NCB concentrated its workshop facilities at Whitwood but it soon became clear that something larger and more modern was required. This took the form of a new Central Workshops which opened in 1959 just to the south of Ledston station, with a ground frame giving rail access from the branch. Part of the new unit's work consisted of maintaining the NCB's considerable fleet of wagons and locomotives. Complete rebuilds were undertaken, but not new locomotive construction. It realised its potential for only a few years before the decline in the mining industry made it increasingly redundant and it closed in the 1980s.

A Hunslet 0 - 6 - 0ST being re-erected inside the shops.
(J Collins)

A typical pre nationalisation workshop was the wagon repair facility for Airedale Collieries at Allerton Bywater, seen in this obviously posed photo from the 1920s.

After overhaul, Hunslet 0-6-0 ST "Airedale" stands outside No 4 bay, resplendent in maroon livery. Rightly proud of their work are (left to right) W Sykes (loco chargehand), J Collins (paint chargehand), G Woodcock (loco fitter and M Lovatt (boilersmith)
(J Collins)

The new Area Central Workshops are in the background as Diesel No 45 moves a varied collection of wagons in 1982. *(J Peden)*

S102 "Cathryn", a Hudswell Clarke product of 1955, in the workshops on 22 March 1969.
(Martin Bairstow collection)

Decline and Fall

For the first seventy years, nothing much changed on the branch – at the northern end, Trench Pit closed in 1930 and an even earlier casualty, in 1905 was Kippax Colliery, neither of which contributed much traffic anyway. Even the withdrawal of passenger trains – few, and lightly loaded, made little difference. Goods services, such as they were, came to an end at Ledston and Kippax stations in 1963 but the real decline set in with great changes in the mining industry. By the end of the 1960s coal exports had virtually disappeared, and oil and gas were rapidly displacing coal as a fuel in home and factory. New coal-fired power stations such as Ferrybridge, Drax and Eggborough didn't compensate for the loss of traditional markets and in any case involved a new pattern of working. This was the 'block' train comprising a set number of permanently-coupled high-capacity hopper wagons designed to run continually between selected collieries equipped with the required loading facilities, and power stations where the train was unloaded automatically without stopping – hence they became known as 'merry-go-rounds'. As all these m.g.r.s were worked off the branch via Castleford, the Bowers to Garforth section became redundant and closed on 14 July 1969.

Primrose Hill colliery ceased production in 1969, supposedly to prolong the lives of Peckfield and Ledston Luck, leaving Allerton Bywater as the only surviving traditional mine.

However, in 1958 the controversial process of opencast mining started in a small way at Astley and after the closure of Primrose Hill, it greatly expanded to include all the area once occupied by the Allerton Main group of collieries, tips and railways. This was designated the St. Aidan's Opencast and some of the coal came out using the Bowers sidings as a railhead, thus ensuring the branch's survival beyond Ledston.

The next casualty was Allerton Bywater, which, though still in production, had its rail connection severed in the mid-1980s and at the same time saw its remaining internal line – to the spoil tips – replaced by a conveyor. A further, and as it turned out, fatal blow came in February 1987 when St. Aidans flooded and remained closed until the late 1990s.

Unexpectedly, after a long period of disuse, the branch came back to life when a loading terminal was established alongside the remains of Ledston station and coal once again flowed by rail from Allerton Bywater, the line beyond having been dismantled.

With no run-round facilities on the branch, empty m.g.r.s arrived from Gascoign Wood and reversed under the control of Castleford Station Box, the loco propelling its train to Allerton. This manoeuvre required an adequately-manned brake van in the rear so that it headed the train when propelling and it was equipped with an 'audible warning device' – a large red bell.

When loaded, the train could then depart with the loco at the head, which it invariably did via the Cutsyke Loop.

Sometimes two trains a day were dealt with in this manner.

The terminal consisted of a small mobile conveyor and a loading shovel but it could load a standard rake of 36 mgr wagons in less than two hours. A brake van is just visible on the end of the

The view south from Ledston bridge in 1977. To the left is the overgrown entrance to the NCB workshops and to the right the stockyards.

40057 and 40077 with a permanent way train at Allerton Bywater about 1982. The train is in a siding, the "main line" being temporarily absent pending renewal. *(Peter Cookson)*

The grandly titled Allerton Bywater Rail Loading Terminal in use on 3 January 1990.

In the last few months of working to Bowers Disposal Point, the track is fighting a losing battle with the undergrowth. 56044 rumbles through the remains of Ledston Station on 5 November 1987.

On 17 September 1987, 56083 treads warily over the level crossing with the Swillington to Allerton road.

Does the sign really say "keep off the grass"? 56083 would find that impossible.

During the final years of operation from Allerton Bywater, inbound empty trains had to be propelled from Castleford. This afforded the unusual sight of a brake van on a train of "merry go round" wagons. When the van was leading, the guard was in radio control with the driver.

train. By this time, to the left of the wagons, a conveyor system occupies the old trackbed to the stockyards and tips.

Reprieve was only temporary and this last source of traffic ended in 1994. Hopes were raised when some sort of loading/unloading facility appeared about 300 yards short of Ledston station but apart from a trial period, it was unused and then dismantled.

Since then, the remains of the LCPJR from East Junction to Ledston station remain in situ though gradually reverting to nature. The site of Allerton Bywater Colliery has been cleared and is the projected home of controversial new development; perhaps the track is being left in place for whatever benefits it might bring in the new railway age. Further north, the trackbed has been turned into a recreational path.

Had the line managed to survive as a through route just a little longer – into the era of the West Yorkshire Passenger Transport Authority, then its fate may have been very different. As to the future, there is physically not much to prevent its re-opening, but this is unlikely (at least as a conventional railway) despite the growth of new housing in the area – there are good park and ride facilities nearby at Garforth.

By converting the trackbed to a cycleway from Garforth to south of Kippax, no buildings obstruct the route and, should funds be available in the distant future, there is little to prevent the re-instatement of a railway, or perhaps more likely, a rapid transit system.

The site of Kippax Station, looking south in early 2000. The track bed has been converted to a cycle way. Trees have hidden the road bridge in the distance and obscured all but the gable end of Station Cottages on the extreme left.